DON CESAR BEACH RESORT

A LOEWS HOTEL

ST PETE BEACH

DON CESAR BEACH RESORT

A LOEWS HOTEL

ST PETE BEACH

A History of The Pink Lady

THE
DONNING COMPANY
PUBLISHERS

"Come all ye who seek health and rest for here they are abundant.'
—Carved in the archway at the Don CeSar's main entrance

Copyright © 2001 by The Don CeSar Beach Resort & Spa
Second printing 2005

For information write:
The Donning Company Publishers
184 Business Park Drive, Suite 206
Virginia Beach, VA 23462

Steve Mull, General Manager
Barbara B. Buchanan, Office Manager
Julia Kilmer-Buitrago, Senior Staff Writer
Richard A. Horwege, Senior Editor
Patricia A. Peterson, Graphic Designer
John Harrell, Imaging Artist
Lynn Walton, Project Research Coordinator
Scott Rule, Director of Marketing

B. L. Walton Jr., Project Director

Library of Congress Cataloging-in-Publication Data

The Don CeSar beach resort & spa : a history of the Pink Lady.
    p. cm.
  ISBN 1-57864-130-6 (alk. paper)
  1. Don CeSar (Saint Pete Beach, Fla.) 2. Hotels—Florida—Saint Pete Beach—History.

  TX941.D68 P56 2001
  647.94759'6301—dc21

2001017233

Printed in the United States of America by Walsworth Publishing Company

Don CeSar Beach Resort
A History of
The Pink Lady

The history of the Don CeSar reads like a marvelous fairy tale. A cast of characters from famous to infamous have strolled the hallways over the past three quarters of a century. There are wartime tales and tales of peace. Tales of financial woes and tales of triumph. Ghost stories and Hollywood glitz. Of course, like any good fairy tale, there is a happy ending.

Through all the changes, one fact remains constant, The Don Ce-Sar (originally hyphenated) with its six tall, pink towers reaching into the Florida sky has been a landmark to the people of St. Pete Beach, Florida, since its grand opening in 1928 and will be for years to come.

The Don Ce-Sar began as an Irishman's dream. Thomas Rowe, an aspiring developer moved to Florida in the early 1920s with dreams of both rebuilding his fragile health and building a luxurious hotel he referred to as his "pink lady." After scouting for a suitable location, Rowe decided on Pass-a-Grille with its white powder sands brushing against the deep azure waters of the Gulf of Mexico. He quickly purchased a strip of land on Long Key between the Gulf and Boca Ciega Bay for the location of his new luxury hotel.

The Don Ce-Sar, Florida's Legendary Pink Palace was built to Thomas Rowe's specifications, blending Moorish and Mediterranean styles of architecture.

Thomas Rowe, founder of the Don Ce-Sar, built the Don as a gift to Florida. Rowe died on the first floor of the Don leaving the property to his estranged wife.

"'I am not looking for any profit' Mr. Rowe said, 'and my only purpose in building the hotel is to give something substantial to the state and island.'" (*Tourist News*, January 9, 1926) Rowe financed the entire project, an act which left him almost destitute, but earned him a place among the who's who of St. Petersburg.

"The first big development north of the city of Pass-a-Grille and probably the most outstanding project on the island, as far as permanent improvements are concerned, is Don-Ce-Sar Place, where Thomas J. Rowe is building his palatial Don Ce-Sar Hotel, probably the greatest structure of its kind on the gulf coast of Florida." (*Tourist News,* January 9, 1926)

Carlton Beard, a local builder, took on the intimidating project of making Rowe's dream into a reality. Along with supervising engineer C. C. Whittaker, Beard constructed the nine-story building. Originally designed as a 225-room hotel, Rowe decided during construction that he wanted a larger building. The final specifications included 325 rooms with private bathrooms and 100 bathing rooms for changing for the beach. There were also 100 staff rooms and a garage with spaces for 100 automobiles. The original opening date for the Don was set as New Year's Day, 1927. According to an article in *Tourist News* dated January 9, 1926, "As the building is more than a third completed now, it will not be necessary to rush the work at the last minute." This prediction was a bit premature as the hotel did not open until 1928.

The Don Ce-Sar, shown here under construction, was built to last. The steel-reinforced ten-inch-thick walls and floors would withstand decades of punishment.

Once completed, the hotel stood as a magnificent structure on the beaches of St. Petersburg with a size-able price tag—$1,150,000. The building was made of Belgian concrete with ten-inch-thick walls and floors. Every eight inches on the floor was criss-crossed with steel rods to maintain the strong structure of the frame. The design of the Don was a combination of Mediterranean and Moorish themes. Stucco and tile walls, red clay tile roofs, arched openings, balconies, and towers on the upper stories added an air of European elegance. Rumor had it that the tall spires were used as a beacon to sailors who traveled the waters of the Gulf of Mexico.

Over the front door, Thomas Rowe had the hotel's greeting carved in an arch: "Come all ye who seek health and rest for here they are abundant." On either side of an arched window above the door stood a pair of lions representing strength. Below the window were a medallion of a ship and a compass rose representing stability.

The hotel's name is derived from the hero Don Caesar de Bazan in the English opera *Maritana.* by musician William Vincent Wallace and playwright Edward Fitzball which opened in London in 1845. They borrowed material from a French play called *Don Caesar de Bazan.* The story was later used as a vehicle for Paramount's *The Spanish Dancer* starring Pola Negri and Adolphe Menjou in the 1920s.

This classic comic opera is set in seventeenth-century Madrid. Spanish King Charles II is captivated by a gypsy girl, Maritana, while Don Jose de Saterem has eyes for the queen. Don Jose sees an opportunity to entrap the king and win the queen for himself, but his first attempts to bring Maritana and King Charles together are foiled because Maritana is above the temptations of wealth and position. He then forms a plan to marry her off to a nobleman to keep her within the palace area and more accessible to the king. His chance comes when Don Caesar de Bazan (the hero of the opera) has been sentenced to death by hanging for dueling during Holy Week (a violation of local ordinance). In the duel, Don Caesar killed a captain of the guard who had abused a young man of the streets called Lazarillo.

Don Jose visits Don Caesar in jail and offers to arrange for him to die by firing squad, a more soldierly death than hanging, if he would marry a noblewoman. Somehow Maritana is tricked and concealed mysteriously beneath a veil and the wedding takes place. Don Caesar is then marched off for execution, but Lazarillo has removed the bullets from the guns and after the smoke clears, Don Caesar finds himself yet alive. Meanwhile, Don Jose, still attempting to play matchmaker between the king and Maritana, has disguised the king as a cavalier. When the king meets Don Caesar and tells him that he is "Don Caesar de Bazan," Don Caesar remarks that he must then be the "king of Spain." The duet, "I Am the King of Spain" and the concurrent sword fight between the two sets the scene for a happy ending.

After the king tells Don Caesar he had previously pardoned him because of his service to the Crown, they justly determined that Don Jose manipulated them to his advantage. In a final attempt to ridicule the king in front of the queen, Don Jose meets his death by Don Caesar's sword. The king appoints him governor of Granada and he and Maritana walk off in happy wedlock.

Although it cannot be certain why Thomas Rowe selected this character for the hotel's name, the nobility of the original Don Ce-Sar has not been lost on the hotel which bears his name. On January 16, 1928, three years and 300 percent over budget, the Don was ready for guests. For the grand opening celebration, more than fifteen hundred guests celebrated the evening in the grand ballroom on the fifth floor with exquisite dining and dancing, for the modest fee of $2.50. Although severely in debt, the Don Ce-Sar began to move towards financial security from opening night. Word of mouth was the best advertisement for the Don, referred to by F. Scott Fitzgerald as a "hotel in an island wilderness" in many of his books. The Don was known throughout the country for its beautiful architecture, exemplary

Don Ce-Sar's Lobby in the 1930s.

service, and tranquil setting. Guests to the Don could request lunch on the beach every day to enjoy the soothing ocean breeze. For a twenty-five-cent service charge, a waiter would set up a table on the beach with an umbrella to provide shade from the strong noon sun and carry food from the fifth floor kitchen for the waiting guests.

Mr. Rowe also provided a variety of entertainment for his guests. A putting green and miniature golf course were installed on the bay side of the building shortly after the hotel's opening. Slot machines were a popular fixture in the first-floor playroom. Some guests were reported to have spent more than $100 in quarters at a single sitting.

One feature which was not present in the original Don was a bar. Aside from the fact that the Don was built during the Prohibition Era, Mr. Rowe was personally opposed to drinking and allowed it only on the first floor. Caving into pressure for a place to get a drink after the repeal of Prohibition, Mr. Rowe added a beverage room in the late 1930s, although he never changed his personal views on alcohol.

On October 28, 1929, the Don, along with the rest of the country, was dealt a serious blow to finances. The stock market, having been driven wild with unchecked speculation purchases, began to falter. By the end of the day the New York Stock Exchange had lost about $4 billion. At the end of the year, the stock market would lose a total of $15 billion dollars. Millionaires became penniless paupers overnight. Although Rowe did not lose the hotel outright in the financial chaos of the Great Depression that followed, financial security was far from certain. There was one saving grace for the Don—the people who could afford to vacation to a luxury hotel enjoyed coming to the Don for its personal touch.

According to Jean Ott, one of Thomas Rowe's employees, "Mr. Rowe thought of the beautiful hotel as his own house and ran it that way. He would sit in a high-backed chair at the top of the stairs in the lobby and survey each guest that registered. If they did not meet his standards, he would request they leave. Just prior to his death he talked of a profit-sharing plan where he would leave part of the hotel to his employees so they could continue to manage it and keep it open after his death."

Unfortunately for the Don and its employees, Thomas Rowe never signed the will which would have implemented the profit-sharing plan. Rowe died of a heart attack on the first floor of the Don in 1940, and his original will left the Don Ce-Sar to his estranged wife, who was less than pleased with her new acquisition. Following the December 7, 1941 attack on Pearl Harbor, almost all 1941–42 season reservations were canceled, and Rowe's widow looked for any excuse to get rid of the Don Ce-Sar property. With the begin-

While maintaining the exterior of a luxury hotel, the Don did have some changes as an Army Air Force Convalescent Hospital. Structures were built on the beach for the training of soldiers. The caption on the back of this photo reads "Don-Ce-Sar Hotel (Station Hosp.) That's where I live, fourth floor."

ing of World War II, she got her wish. In desperate need for properties to house soldiers in training, the US government began to purchase hotel properties around the state of Florida. During the war years, one out of every three hotels in the state of Florida was purchased by the Army. The Army got a great bargain with the Don. It was lost by Mrs. Rowe for back taxes and purchased by the government for $450,000.

The first governmental use of the Don was as a sub base hospital for McDill Field. Soon afterwards, the federal government decided to utilize the Don as a Convalescent Hospital. The first troops to staff the facility arrived in July of 1942. Originally Lieutenant Colonel Jacob J. Spencer, commanding officer and surgeon and Captain Nathan Botwin, adjutant were in charge of the enormous task of converting the hotel to a hospital facility to serve the Basic Training Centers for St. Petersburg. On the average, the Don Ce-Sar Hospital answered eight hundred sick calls every day during 1942. The first patient was recorded as a flyer who fell down after getting out of his plane. In 1943, when it was a convalescent hospital, eighteen hundred sick calls were being received daily from the surrounding area. As the war years went on, the Don also was used to treat psychiatric issues such as combat fatigue.

Visitors and the Don Roger *helped to keep morale high at the Don Ce-Sar AAF Convalescent Hospital.*

The facility had its own newsletter, the *Don Roger*—*Don* for the Don Ce-Sar facility and *Roger* for the military code meaning "message received." The name, suggested by Staff Sergeant Edward P. McNulty, was chosen from hundreds of entries in a name the newsletter contest. A cash prize of ten dollars was awarded for the winning entry. The new name replaced the original name, *Don Ce-Sarian*, which first appeared on September 15, 1943. Managing editor Technical Sergeant Charles M. Nekvasil compiled articles on everything from war news to pin-up photographs shot on the St. Petersburg Beach. According to Colonel Richard E. Elvins, the hospital commanding officer, "*Don Roger* is a newspaper worthy of the Don Ce-Sar, and stacks up with the best organs of its kind in the entire Air Force." (*Don Roger*, February 19, 1945)

The *Don Roger* tackled a variety of issues in its short run. One of the more interesting repeat stories played out in the announcements section and concerned the loss of soda bottles. . . .

"The Post Exchange at Don Ce-Sar has been losing a lot [of] coke bottles lately, as well as other types. The Post Exchange officer would appreciate everyone who takes bottles out of the exchange to return them as promptly as possible." (*Don Roger*, August 4, 1945)

"The Post Exchange is rapidly losing a lot of coke bottles, which for some reason or other continue to walk out of the place. Be sure you always return yours!" (*Don Roger*, September 8, 1945)

FINAL!!   FINAL!!

Ray Melville, Eden Nicholas Star In "Pardon Me" Oct. 1st

Ray Melville, and Eden Nicholas, two of America's greatest Musical Comedy stars, will appear at the Don, Monday evening, October 1st, at 8:15 p. m., heading a cast of nearly 35 entertainers, plus an intimate orchestra group, to present the Musical show, PARDON ME.

The revue, brought to the Don, following a tour of the legitimate theatres in the East, is complete with a line of dancing girls, and carries its own musical ensemble.

The scene is set in the hotel lobby of a small lodge in the heart of the Maine woods. Complications set in, when Mr. Nicholas, as an author with his mind set on fishing, and his secretary, Mr. Melville, are taken for each other, by the proprietress .. a keen fisherwoman herself, who is obviously trying to hook a man for her daughter. The daughter, in defiance, pretends to be one of the maids which should give you some idea of the merry mixup.

About this plot are woven the tunes of the revue, "I've Done It Again," and "i Want To Dance." Both are of hit calibre and sung by Nicholas and Melville.

Music for the show was written by Edward Edwards, and lyrics by A. Seymour Brown. Dances are under the direction of Sandy Grant, while Harry A. Krivit keeps the whole production moving backstage.

The musical ensemble is under Joseph Garnett, Broadway maestro, and curtain time is 8:15 p. m.

Departures

Captain Edmond Weglarz, Mess Officer of the Don is being transferred to the AAF Convalescent Hospital, Plattsburg Barracks, New York.

Captain Carel Van Der Heide, recently returned from TDY in Europe, has been transferred to the AAF Regional and Convalescent Hospital, Santa Ana, California.

S/Sgt. Edward McNulty Won Contest Naming Paper Last February

S/SGT. EDWARD P. McNULTY, of Brooklyn, N. Y., was winner of the contest held to name the "Don Roger" when the first paper came off the press and was delivered to personnel here on February 10, 1945.

The name "Don Roger" was selected from over 250 entries, including such titles as "Don Fence Me In," "Donvalescent," "Don Formula," "Mastodon," "Don Salvage," "Donology," "Don Eye-Piece," "Don Annals," "Don Mirror," and "Don Legend."

Dear Mr. Anthony:

I can't get out on a Section 8 because I can count up to 8. Can't get out on a CDD because when they shake me nothing falls out. Can't get a Section 9 for being inadaptable to Army Chow. Too old to fight but not old enough to get out on the over 35 rule. Can't get out on points I only have 41. What I want to know Mr. Anthony, is "How does a fellow go about being declared a Surplus War Commodity." Please answer before San Antonio.

       Sincerely,
         Would-be Civilian (or should that be Won't-be Civilian?)

Don Provides Shelter For 400 Islanders In Hurricane Alert

"As always, Don Ce-Sar stands ready to succor the distressed." This statement by Major Winfred Post, commanding officer of the Don went out over the air waves and was reprinted in emergency issues of all St. Petersburg papers as the 143 mile an hour destructive hurricane cut its deadly arc toward this area, last Saturday, September 15th.

Shortly after 10 p. m. the vanguard of 400 refugees from the Gulf Beaches began pouring into the hospital in response to orders from local relief agencies to evacuate the islands. Instantly, every available motor vehicle from the Don pool was pressed into service to bring in the aged and crippled persons to shelter.

For 24 hours preceding the blow, the Post Engineers worked feverishly to make the building ready to withstand the heavy winds and possible high tide. Windows were boarded and as the shelterers began to stream in, crews of permanent party began placing mattresses in the theatre auditorium and in the main lobby.

Further Precautions Taken

Following reports at midnight that the storm was increasing in intensity, leaving heavy damage in its path, further precautions were taken to provide emergency rescue service and immediate medical aid anywhere along the beach area, if necessary. Ambulance crews were briefed for emergency procedure, and from a map set up in the Post Headquarters, the path of the storm and its center were pinpointed hourly from late reports. Women with infant children were bedded down while other civilians and dependents of military personnel slept on mattresses on the main floor or in

(Continued on Page 5)

Major Winfred L. Post, M.C.
Commanding Officer

The Don Roger *provided a variety of news for its military residents. Everything from church attendance rosters to humorous stories from the front lines appeared in its thirty-one issues.*

Many famous visitors came to the Don during the war years to build the morale of the troops being treated. Among the famous guests were Joe DiMaggio, and Cary Grant.

As the war drew to a close, rumors began flying about the possibility of closing the hospital. The first rumors of closing were brought up in June of 1945. In September of 1945, the *Don Roger* tackled the issue of the possible closing. "The 'in-again out-again Finnegan' status of the hospital has been just that since the early days of June this year. At that time rumors were floating in the high tides of the Gulf of Mexico, and the expected closing then was August 15, 1945."

Holidays were especially difficult on servicemen. To create a home away from home, the Don provided a traditional Thanksgiving meal of roast young turkey, sage stuffing, and spiced pumpkin pie in 1943.

Cary Grant (right) was one of many celebrities to visit the Don during both war and peace. Also pictured are Colonel Howard A. Rusk, AAF Chief of Convalescent Training (left) and Colonel Richard E. Elvins, hospital commanding officer (center).

Before the end of 1945, the last patients were sent home and the hospital was converted to Veterans Administration (VA) offices. As time went by, the VA offices began to move to other locations only to be replaced by other federal tenants. The last of the VA offices left in 1962.

The federal offices remained in use for the next seven years. In the early 1960s, the federal government decided to start moving a majority of the federal offices closer to downtown. Slowly the offices were moved from the Don to new locations. One reason for the move was the lack of air conditioning in the Don. The federal government determined that it would be more cost-effective to move the offices than to install air conditioning units throughout the Don. As the last of the offices moved out in 1969, the Don was left empty—a silent tribute to the past.

A treasured memento—one of the last views of the Don Ce-Sar AAF Convalescent Hospital.

Restoration of the Don was a massive undertaking with a mammoth price tag—more than $3 million.

What to do with the Don was a hot topic for many years. Restoration with private ownership or demolition with public usage were some of the ideas considered.

After being home to the AAF Convalescent Hospital and VA offices for more than two decades, the Don became St. Petersburg's "Pink Elephant." For locals, the Don was still an impressive backdrop as shown in this 1968 photograph from across the Bay.

Over the years, the vacant building began to deteriorate and soon became a shattered shell of its former glory. The paint began to peel from exposure to the sun and salty sea air. The windows were shattered and the hotel became a home only for vagrants and curious onlookers. Out of the 13,900 panes of glass, an average of 5 panes of glass shattered daily. The Don Ce-Sar had earned a new nickname—the Pink Elephant. The *St. Petersburg Independent* lamented, "Sitting like a big stucco wedding cake overlooking the Gulf of St. Petersburg Beach, it merely gathers dust and age, rats and other vermin, a few aimless tenants willing to chance a run-in with the law, assorted lovers, and growing disrepair." (*St. Petersburg Independent*, February 2, 1971) Unwanted by the federal and local governments, it looked like the Don would be slated for the wrecking ball.

Ironically, Thomas Rowe's desire for a building which would withstand the test of time may have bought enough time to save the Don. The building, which had withstood hurricanes with only minor damage, would take a considerable amount of money to demolish. One early estimate placed the cost of demolition at $50,000, although that estimate was soon deemed far too low.

Shattered windows and peeling paint gave the Don more eyesore than elegance in the early 1970s.

In 1971, a small group of citizens formed a "Save the Don" committee. According to an article by the *St. Petersburg Beach Register*, June Hurley Young and her 'Save the Don' committee "is searching every avenue open to establish a responsible group of investors to refurbish the Don for use as a magnificent hotel, convention hall with its grand ballroom [to] the grand and stately era of splendor . . . [as] an exciting challenge?" The twelve-member committee was composed of Paul Resop (chairman), Mrs. J. Kenneth Hurley (vice chair), Mrs. Fred Wisskup (secretary), Carol Curotto (owner of the Bon Aire motel), Mrs. James Merritt (owner of Sun-Sea motel), John Fairfield (architect), Percy Meeker (retired businessman and columnist), Bush Locknane (retired FDA official), Ray Martin (editor/publisher of the *Pinellas Review*), Ed Stanton (retired contractor), W. J. Ruscoe (president of the Don Ce-Sar property owners), and Mrs. Virginia Harris (former member of the Beautification Committee of HUD).

When the Don was given to the government for use, the first-floor fountain was removed. When restoration began in the 1970s, a note was found—a plea that the fountain be restored. The date on the letter, month and day, was the same as the date when the fountain site was exposed during renovation twenty-five years later.

Modern amenities, such as air conditioning, had to be included in the restoration project in addition to removing the signs of age from the hotel. The restoration of the Don essentially gutted the inside and built new walls (left) and new decorative features (right).

Once completed, the Don was once again a masterpiece of elegance and grace on St. Petersburg's coast.

William Bowman and Beach Resorts International became the new owners for the Don around the middle of February 1972 for the modest price tag of $460,000. Now it was time for the restoration to begin. The restoration was going to be costly. An early estimate concluded that the restoration project would cost around three and a half million dollars. Approximately ninety plumbers, air conditioning technicians, carpenters, and electrician's worked on the restoration of the Don. In the end, restoration would cost $7.5 million, but would bring the value of the hotel and property to $30 million.

Although the Don was going to resemble the original 1928 structure as much as possible, there were a few notable changes. First, air conditioning would be added throughout the Don providing exceptional comfort to the guests. Second, the name was to change. Originally called the *Don Ce-Sar*, the restoration committee opted to remove the hyphen in 1972 leaving the *Don Ce Sar*, as it is called today.

Finally, after nearly two years of work, the Don CeSar reopened on November 24 of 1973. With a glorious reopening party, it looked like the Don was back as a permanent fixture in the St. Pete Beach shoreline. The Don was listed on the National Register of Historic Places in 1974 and a marker placed at street level with a large copy on the Garden floor near the spa and fitness room to commemorate this significant event.

On the surface, the future looked bright for the Don. Dark clouds were looming on the horizon, however. A troubled economy created financial trouble for the Don. By 1975, the Don was in serious financial shape. William Bowman lost the Don CeSar on his birthday—October 24, 1975, after he had completed $6 million of renovations. Hospitality Management Corporation of Dallas was immediately hired to help sort out the financial difficulties, including liens of $175,000 by the Internal Revenue Service. As the financial condition of the Don improved, the hotel was transferred to the Don Ce Sar Resort Hotel Ltd., a partnership made of Connecticut General Life Insurance Company and Connecticut General Mortgage and Realty Investments. By 1978 the Don was back in the black.

Daniel F. Gifford
Vice President and General Manager
Don CeSar Beach Resort Hotel
requests the pleasure of your company
at a Birthday Luncheon celebrating
the 50th Anniversary of
the Don CeSar Beach Resort Hotel
Monday, the sixteenth of January
nineteen hundred and seventy-eight
commencing at eleven-thirty
with Cocktails and Ceremonies
followed by Lunch
3400 Gulf Boulevard
St. Petersburg Beach, Florida

R.S.V.P.   Please present this invitation

The Don celebrated its fiftieth anniversary in style with an exquisite luncheon in 1978.

The Don of 1978 was restored to the glory of Thomas Rowe's vision.

The Don CeSar—A haunted hotel?

More than thirty years after his death, some employees say that Mr. Rowe has returned. According to a variety of newspaper articles, television shows, and personal interviews, strange happenings have been occurring since the reopening of the Don in 1973. Gerard Faille, a cleaning man at the Don in the mid-1970s, claims to have seen the ghost of Thomas Rowe on several occasions. As Rowe's visitations increased in frequency, Faille reported receiving notes left behind by Rowe as the guardian of the Don. Other employees have reported cold chills, the sight of an elderly man in a white suit and a Panama hat, and glasses sliding down the bar and breaking on the wall. While skeptics may scoff at the idea, there are hundreds of believers who are certain that the Don has one extra special guest roaming the halls at night.

Although the movie Health *did not make a great impression at box offices, the filming at the Don made an interesting experience for guests.*

From February 20 to March 30, 1979, the Don hosted the filming crew of the movie *Health*. Although the movie did not fare well at the box office, the Don provided an elegant set for the filming. Many guests to the Don can recall meeting stars such as Lauren Bacall, Carol Burnett, James Garner, and Glenda Jackson.

During the late 1970s and early 1980s, the Don got a dramatic face lift. The King Charles Restaurant was refurbished in 1979, and remodeling of the penthouse was completed in 1980. To add additional dining options, Le Bistro opened on February 15, 1980. One of the most dramatic redecorating changes occurred in the Grand Ballroom. According to the Summer 1980 newsletter, "Starting with the Grand Ballroom, carpeting, draperies, and wallpaper will add a new dimension to our decor. Following the ballroom, redecorating will take place at the registration desk in the lobby, King Charles Restaurant on the fifth floor, and suites throughout the hotel. Then our second penthouse will be completely refurnished and hopefully all will be completed by the end of October."

The 1980s was a time of exciting events at the Don. The sandcastle contest was an annual favorite, bringing amateurs to professional sand sculptors to the pristine Gulf beach. On April 18, 1980, the Don hosted the John Eastman radio show which broadcast a live show, the first of many live broadcasts. Other events graced the Don during the 1980s. A hair-braiding contest displayed the works of a variety of hair artists on June 28, 1981. A Jet Ski Championship brought skilled performers to the Gulf waters and beaches of the Don from August 29 to 30, 1981. The Don's softball team won the title after a 25–6 victory over the Happy Dolphin team in 1981. The softball team was composed entirely of employees. On the literary scene, *National Geographic* honored the Don with a gorgeous color photograph in its August 1982 edition.

In 1982, the Don received another famous guest. Florida Governor Bob Graham made a visit to the Don and utilized the Grand Ballroom for delivery of a speech. Governor Graham wasn't the only guest to use the backdrop of the Don to make an impression. Tom Petty and the Heartbreakers filmed an MTV video special at the Don in 1985. Ad agencies also enjoyed the splendor of the Don for model photo shoots. Dillards, Ivey's, and many others photographed fashion models against the breathtaking architecture of the Don CeSar.

The Lobby Bar in 1979, complete with fountain and a variety of tropical plants.

As the fall of 1982 neared to a close, the Don once again provided the backdrop for another major motion picture. *Once Upon a Time in America*, starring Robert DeNiro, James Woods, and Tuesday Weld, told the story of guests staying at a grand hotel during and after the repeal of Prohibition.

Throughout the 1980s the one constant at the Don was change. Sections of the hotel were restored and re-restored to try and accomplish a perfect tribute to Mr. Rowe's somewhat eccentric design. For example, the Don has a hidden staircase that seemingly rises two flights only to end up going nowhere. One problem that restoration crews did not have to face was the need for repairs to the foundation. Since its construction, the foundation of the Don CeSar has remained without any cracks or damage.

More renovations were needed in the mid-1980s. This photograph shows the fifth-floor Del Prado Hall in 1986 prior to renovation.

The King Charles Restaurant also underwent renovations in 1986.

The renovation process
covered every inch of
the Don—from ceiling
(above) to floor (left).

As each section was com-
pleted, a ribbon-cutting
gala heralded the
reopening of a new area.

Mr. Charles W. Lanphere,
Chairman and President
of Hospitality Management Corporation
and Mr. Luis Marco, General Manager
of the Don CeSar Beach Resort
respectfully request your presence
at the celebration of
A MASTERPIECE RESTORED

From Friday, January 30, 1987
to Sunday, February 1, 1987,
the Don CeSar Beach Resort will
celebrate its Grand Re-Opening with
fireworks and special events.

For the past 18 months,
skilled craftsmen have worked
to return the Don CeSar
to its original elegance.
Completely new bedrooms,
bathrooms, public areas, ballrooms
and meeting facilities.

We look forward to having you with us as
a special guest for this celebration.

RSVP Card Enclosed
Invitation for Two

THE
Don Ce Sar
BEACH RESORT

3400 Gulf Boulevard
St. Petersburg Beach, Florida 33706
813/360-1881

After eighteen months of restoration, the Don reopened as "A Masterpiece Restored."

An artist's conception of the new Don, presented by Beach Resorts International, Inc. president William Bowman Jr. and architect Robert D. Vodicka.

One of the trademarks of the Don CeSar is the bright pink color of the hotel's exterior. Since the hotel is located on the ocean, saltwater corrosion and the bright Florida sun can do a considerable amount of damage to the color of a building. Every five years, the Don must be repainted to maintain its pink coloration. The original color is called Don CeSar Pink, according to specifications from the original supplier, Coranado Paint. It takes approximately nine months to spread the twelve thousand gallons of paint on the exterior of the Don, but as one local citizen commented, "It just wouldn't be the Don if it wasn't pink."

THE Don CeSar BEACH RESORT
St. Petersburg Beach

Florida's Showplace

If you dreamed a hotel, it would be this one.

Brochures since 1970 reflect the changing styles of the decades.

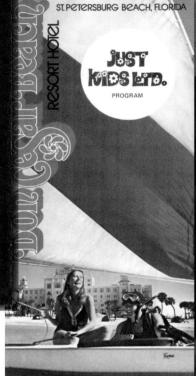

DON CeSar BEACH RESORT HOTEL

ST. PETERSBURG BEACH, FLORIDA

JUST KIDS LTD.
PROGRAM

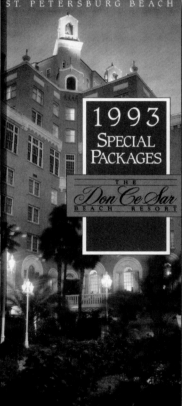

ST. PETERSBURG BEACH

1993 SPECIAL PACKAGES

THE Don CeSar BEACH RESORT

In 1992, a new management company was brought in, Interstate Hotels Corporation who continued the tradition of excellence. In 1997, the Don added a new property under its ownership. Located a brief quarter mile to the north of the Don is the Beach House Suites by The Don CeSar. While the Beach House is a less formal setting, the seventy-suite facility still maintains the high luxury of a European retreat. In addition to reflecting the quality service and atmosphere of the Don, the Beach House shares another similarity with its parent building—the exterior of the Beach House's five stories are resplendent in Don CeSar pink.

Throughout its history, the Don CeSar has remained true to Thomas Rowe's vision. The Don of today exemplifies the finest in resort luxury. The elegant exterior is mirrored in its interior halls. With English Axminster carpets, French candelabras, and Italian crystal chandeliers, the Don captures the grace of European design while maintaining a casual American ambiance. Additionally, the Don CeSar offers a wide variety of amenities to its guests. From a luxurious day spa to exhilarating water sports, there's always something new to try at the Don.

The future of the Don looks filled with promise as well. With the completion of another major restoration in January 2001, the Don CeSar has once again reached the highest level of quality for visitors from around the world. The motto first posted by Thomas Rowe almost three-quarters of a century ago still rings true today: "Come all ye who seek health and rest for here they are abundant."

St. Pete Beach, Florida

Don CeSar Resort Hotel

A Return to Elegance

Don CeSar Resort Hotel
3400 Gulf Beach Blvd./St. Petersburg Beach, FL. 33706
Telephone: 813/360-1881

The **DON CeSAR** A REGISTRY RESORT

ISLAND FUN & SUN

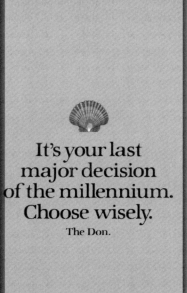

It's your last major decision of the millennium. Choose wisely.

The Don.

Snapshots of the Pink Lady
Amenities offered at the Don CeSar

A modern Don.

The Don CeSar Spa: Nothing can make a vacation into the ultimate relaxing experience more than a trip to the Spa. At the Don a blending of European techniques and exotic botanicals create an experience to remember. Some of the treatments offered are based on European Thalassotherapy which utilizes the healing properties of sea products. One of the most popular treatments is the Sun Soother, designed to replenish lost moisture from the skin with an emollient of sea plant extracts, sandalwood, and lavender. Other offerings include wraps, massage, and a state-of-the-art fitness facility.

The Garden Level and Boardwalk Shoppes: Located on the Garden Level, the Shoppes offer a variety of unique boutiques for the discerning shopper. At DeBazan, shoppers can select from the latest in designer sportswear for men and women. Need to change for the pool? Splash features quality swimwear for the whole family. Getting ready for a stylish evening out? London Hair provides a full range of hair, nail, and skin care services. For an added touch of elegance, try Ronay Jewelers. Also located in the Boardwalk Shoppes are TR's General Store, offering a wide variety of specialty items and florals. Lastly, to commemorate your stay, visit the Don CeSar Logo Shoppe for exclusive Don merchandise. With so many exciting offerings, the Boardwalk Shoppes are truly a shopper's paradise.

The Garden Level also offers special activities periodically. Check with the concierge's desk for the current special events at the Don.

The lobby gives guests a stunning first impression of the Don.

*The lobby arcade is a sunny
spot for work or relaxation.*

*The Grand Ballroom (left) is one of a dozen rooms
providing elegant settings for corporate meetings
or social functions (below).*

*The annual sandcastle contest brought artists from around the state to
build a variety of sculptures, including a sand version of the United States Seal.*

Water sports provide hours of entertainment for guests to the Don. Water skiing, jet skiing, parasailing, and surfing are some of the more popular Gulf sports.

Golf is one of the popular local activities conveniently located near to the Don CeSar at Isla Del Sol.

Activities: If you're looking to add some excitement to your time at the Don, there are plenty of activities in store. Some offerings include workshops on body toning, dancing, and yoga. For one-on-one interaction, try a workout with your own personal trainer. Group activities like volleyball and water aerobics are always fun for all. There are even activities for the kids including nature walks, sandcastle building, scavenger hunts, and arts and crafts. Of course the Gulf of Mexico also provides its own entertainment. The Don offers sailboats, catamarans, aquabikes, kayaks, fishing, parasailing, golfing, snorkeling, and scuba diving. Whatever your fancy, the Don CeSar has the perfect afternoon diversion waiting for you.

Jet-ski competitions (above) and fashion shows (below) draw large crowds to the pristine waters and beaches of the Don.

The sugar-white beach and warm Florida Sun welcome guests to The Don. Take advantage of one of the world's most celebrated beaches. Slip into your bathing suit and plunge into the clear, blue Gulf. Spend the day wave-running, sailing, aqua-biking, windsurfing, fishing, scuba-diving, snorkeling, or just share the sun with someone special. Come dip into one of our two large pools. One is four feet deep and perfect for group activities such as aqua-aerobics or water volleyball. The second pool features an underwater sound system. The not-too-faint-at-heart can parasail, and for those who prefer to keep their feet on the ground, there's beach volleyball. Team sports are great activities at meetings and attendees can take advantage of special leadership and confidence-building programs like our Beach Olympics. Complimentary shuttle service is available to take you to a neighboring championship golf course and tennis facilities. Just name your interest and our Concierge or Conference Service Department will make all your arrangements, including dinner cruises, sports and theater tickets. Our counselors at Kids, Ltd. will gladly take care of your children, ages five to twelve, with supervised games and activities. We also offer a fully equipped Beach Club and Spa with sauna, whirlpool, professional masseuses, and trainers on staff.

The Maritana Grille on the Lobby level.

Restaurants: One highlight of any vacation should be dining in world-class style. At the Don CeSar, a wide range of restaurants cater to even the most discriminating palate. The Maritana Grille, a four-diamond restaurant located on the Lobby level, offers a tantalizing menu in an exotic setting. Surrounded by fifteen hundred gallons of saltwater aquariums filled with indigenous Florida fish, the Maritana Grille offers a friendly atmosphere where jackets are definitely not required. For an intimate experience, reserve the Chef's Table at the Maritana Grille. Watch as elegant entrees are prepared before your eyes by Executive Chef Eric Neri and his staff. If your idea of relaxation involves watching the sun sink slowly into the Gulf, try dinner at the Sea Porch Café. The Sea Porch Café also offers breakfast and lunch fare, served with everything from tropical fruits to fresh seafood. For a casual lunch or snack, the Beachcomber Grill, located next to the pool area, provides light meals in a relaxed setting. For an evening nightcap, Sunsets' and the Lobby Bar both offer a complete selection from fine wine to draft beer and cigars. Sunday brunch is offered in the former King Charles Restaurant, now the King Charles Ballroom with over 180 different items. Sunday Brunch is not to be missed! Finally, Uncle Andy's Ice Cream Parlour is one of the best ways to beat the Florida heat. Whatever type of food you desire, the Don CeSar has the finest selection available.

APPETIZERS:

Maine Lobster Agnolotti Pasta with Wilted Leeks,
Coral Butter and White Truffle Oil 10.50

Prosciutto Wrapped Prawns with Capellini Pasta,
Grilled Vidalia Onions and Parsley 12.75/26.75

Five Spiced Seared Breast of Duck on Glazed
Pineapple, Ginger Risotto and Soy Broth 12.25

Tequila and Key Lime Cured Salmon, Dikon Salad,
Vegetable Tuna Roll, Margarita Vinaigrette 11.75

Pan Seared Sea Scallop with Leek and Mushroom
Fricassee, Beluga Caviar and
Parsley Butter 11.75

Roasted Portobello Mushroom with Duck and
Artichoke Hash, Foie Gras, Castello Cheese
and Port Glaze 12.50

Beluga Caviar with Maritana Breads
Market Price

SALADS:

Maritana Caesar with Potato Croutons
8.50

Warm Tossed Field Greens with Castello Cheese,
Spicy Glazed Pecans and Roasted Shallot, Pancetta
Vinaigrette 8.75

Heirloom Tomato Carpaccio and Micro Green Salad
with Red Onion and Basil Vinaigrette
Market Price

Yellow Fin Potato and Herbed Goat Cheese
Terrine with Micro Greens, Truffle
and Beet Essence 9.50

*We are proud to use local and organic produce
whenever possible.*

*The Chef will gladly accommodate
any special dietary needs!*

**WE OFFER A SMOKE FREE DINING ROOM,
THANK YOU FOR NOT SMOKING.**

ENTREES:

Horseradish Crusted Atlantic Salmon with Shrimp
Fricassee and Lobster Butter 26.50

Pan Seared Calico Bay Cod with Lobster Risotto,
Roasted Cepes and Shellfish Broth 28.50

Seared Ahi Tuna with Asian Mango and Fennel Salad,
Florida Citrus and Crab Vinaigrette 28.50

Marmalade Roasted Gulf Red Snapper with Pea Vine
Salad, Sweet Potato Gnocchi and Mandarin Orange
Vinaigrette 26.50

Pan Seared Sea Scallops & Wood Grilled Breast of
Duck with Porcini Mushroom, Leek Salad and
Roasted Corn Demi 27.50

Orange Habanero BBQ Gulf Fish with Grilled
Hawaiian Pineapple, Wilted Greens and
Rum Pepper Paint 27.50

Pan Seared Chilean Sea Bass with Papaya Banana
Ravioli, Petite Salad, Crispy Salsify
and Coral Butter 27.50

FROM OUR WOOD BURNING GRILL:

Grilled Filet Mignon with Horseradish Mashed
Potatoes, Candied Shallots, Tomato Confit
and Tawny Port Glaze 29.50

Wood Grilled Colorado Lamb Rack with Roasted Pearl
Onions, English Peas, Artichokes, Truffle Mashed and
Rosemary Cabernet Reduction 31.50

Wood Grilled Venison Loin with Warm Roasted
Eggplant and Mushroom Salad, Truffle Mashed and
Foie Gras Infused Demi 31.75

INTRODUCING THE AREA'S ONLY CHEF'S TABLE

Located in the kitchen area, guests are able to
interact with our chefs for the ultimate dining
experience. We are accepting reservations now for
groups of 4-8 persons. See Ryszard Jurkiewicz, our
Maitre D', for availability.

After your dinner, may we suggest our desserts
veranda, where you will find a grand selection of
desserts, cognacs, single-malt scotches and cigars.

House specialties from the Maritana Grille combine the best of Florida seafood with exotic seasonings.

The Chefs at the Don create masterpieces of food every day.
Fresh seafood from local waters is expertly prepared daily.

Bountiful food served with style is one of many trademarks of the Don.

Children frolic in one of the Don's pools.

Uncle Andy's Ice Cream Parlour offers dozens of flavors in a 1950s soda-counter setting.
Uncle Andy's is located at the original entrance to the Don on the Garden Level.

The Catering Staff at the Don provides food for a variety of occasions.
Ice sculptures and creative displays are coordinated to accommodate any occasion.

More than three hundred weddings are held every year at the Don. The chefs and catering department can accommodate any request from a special wine list to a six-tier wedding cake.

Weddings, Conventions, and Special Events: What better location for a wedding than a seaside castle? Want to have a convention that caters both to style and convenience? The Don CeSar staff are specialists in making your event extraordinary. When you decide to host an event at the Don CeSar, you will be given star treatment and the extra special care that makes your dream become a reality. The Don CeSar hosts more than three hundred weddings every year. For business functions, the Don offers eight conference rooms and five outdoor waterside arenas to impress attendees. For social functions, the Don are specialists in creative parties. Some parties in the past have included a Great Gatsby Celebration (complete with appearances by Al Capone and F. Scott Fitzgerald), Shipwrecked Survivors (with a buffet of shrimp, oysters, and crabs legs), and a Polynesian Luau (featuring a roasted pig, fire dancers, and tiki torches). Regardless of your needs, the Don CeSar staff is ready and willing to make any event an incredible experience.

Halloween wouldn't be complete without a haunted tour, especially with the legend of Thomas Rowe's ghost drifting through the halls.

Theme events, such as Circus Night, provide evenings of entertainment for visitors to the Don.

The lobby bar provides a relaxing atmosphere for socializing.

The Grand Ballroom becomes a different hall—the ballroom of the HMS Titanic.

Other theme events turn the hallways of the Don into back alleys of 1920s Chicago.

Egypt comes to Florida with a King Tut event. The Grand Ballroom becomes an Egyptian treasure trove (above) as guests are greeted by a full-size sarcophagus.

The grounds around the Don are a work of art with a blend of tropical palm trees and blooming flowers.

Poolside relaxation in the shadow of the Pink Castle is a popular activity year-round.

A visit to the Don begins by the arrival at the front driveway entrance with valet parking. The front entrance opens onto the first floor, one floor above the street level.

The forty guest suites and twin two-story penthouses provide additional features from a small living room with a fireplace to a second private bedroom. This is the Presidential Suite.

The Don has 277 guest rooms featuring a variety of amenities from goose-down pillows to complimentary terry bathrobes. Room service offers gourmet meals without leaving the comfort of your guest room.

The beach is a beautiful place to share moments together.

Sunset at the Don turns a swimming pool into a reflecting pool.

Catered private dining opportunities include the Pavilion and the King Charles Ballroom.

There is nothing like a good massage at the Don's spa.

The Don's Beach House.

The Chefs utilize only the freshest ingredients in creation of their daily specialties.

Banquet service offers culinary masterpieces with an attractive ambiance.

Restaurant dining ranges from casual at the Sea Porch Café to elegant at the Maritana Grille.

Summer Rates
for 1974–1975

Singles—$18–26
Doubles—$22–30
Efficiencies—$28–34
1-Bedroom Suite—$34–50
Deluxe suite—$44–50
Penthouse—$250
Lunch in the King Charles Room—$1.95
Dinner—$5.95

Summer Rates
for 1991–1992

Single/Double—$115–135
Jr. Suite—$195
1 Bedroom/1 Bath—$210–225
1 Bedroom/2 Bath—$375–395
2 Bedroom—$375–395
Penthouse—$600

Summer Rates
for 1999–2000

Single/Double—$219–249
Jr. Suite—$289–319
1 Bedroom/1Bath—$379–409
1 Bedroom/2 Bath—$494–509
2 Bedroom—$574
Penthouse—$1250–1500

Famous guests to the Don include (but certainly aren't limited to):

Andre Agassi
Robert Altman
Paul Anka
Ann Margaret
Chet Atkins
Lauren Bacall
Tony Bennett
George Benson
Jon Bon Jovi
Anita Bryant
Jimmy Buffett
Carol Burnett
President George Bush
President Jimmy Carter
Lynda Carter
Dick Cavett
Carol Channing
Cher
Dick Clark
Hilary Rodham Clinton
President Bill Clinton
Alistair Cook
Kevin Costner
Clarence Darrow
Robert DeNiro
Dixie Chicks
Michael Douglas
Duran Duran
Dr. Wayne Dyer
Sheena Easton
Farrah Fawcett
Joseph Finnes
F. Scott Fitzgerald
President Gerald Ford
Harrison Ford
Eva Gabor

Zsa Zsa Gabor
James Garner
Lou Gehrig
Barry Gibb
Dr. Jane Goodall
Grateful Dead
Wayne Gretsky
Dr. Clarence Hall
Scot Hamilton
Mariel Hemmingway
Charlton Heston
Hulk Hogan
Glenda Jackson
Elton John
Don Johnson
Emmett Kelly Sr.
Coretta Scott King
Jeanne Kirkpatrick
Henry Kissinger
Heidi Klum
Ann Landers
Jerry Lewis
Ray Liotta
Sophia Loren
Barry Manilow
Mickey Mantle
Dan Marino
Dave Matthews
Dr. Walter Mayo
Patrick McNee
Bette Midler
Gretchen Moll
Joe Montana
Wayne Newton
Jack Nicholson
Stevie Nicks

Tom Petty
Pink Floyd
Tom Poston
Anthony Quinn
Rob Reiner
Janet Reno
Burt Reynolds
President Franklin D. Roosevelt
Mark Russell
Babe Ruth
Sade
Laurie Lee Schaeffer
Paul Schrader
Steven Seigel
Tom Selleck
Doc Severinsen
Dinah Shore
Brittany Spears
Rick Springfield
Susan St. James
Ringo Starr
Rod Stewart
Sally Struthers
Elizabeth Taylor
James Taylor
Lowell Thomas
Kathleen Turner
Barbara Walters
Tom Watson
Tuesday Weld
Dr. Elie Wiesel
Joe Williams
James Woods
Kristi Yamaguchi
Ephrem Zimbelist Jr.

The Don CeSar has blended elegance with excellence for more than seven decades.

Awards and Acclaims

Here is a small sampling of the numerous awards received by the Don CeSar and the Maritana Grille with The Chef's Table.

AAA Four Diamond Rating (nineteen years in a row)

Mobil Four Star

Zagat Survey—Extraordinary

Southern Living—Favorite Beach Resort Hotel Reader's Choice Award

Gourmet Magazine—Distinctive Restaurants of Florida

Insurance Conference Planner—Premium Circle Award

Wine Spectator—Award of Excellence

Epicurean Rendezvous—One of the Top 100 Restaurants in Florida

Medical Meetings—Merit & Distinction Award

Meetings South—Stars of the South Award

Spa Magazine—Ritziest Spot in Town

Florida Trend—Golden Spoon Award, Top 200

Florida Hotel & Motel Journal—Golden Key

Tampa Bay Magazine—Best New Restaurant Idea

Successful Meetings—Pinnacle Award

National Register of Historic Places

National Trust for Historic Preservation

Historic Hotels of America

Sources

The Don CeSar has been displayed on many occasions through magazine and newspaper articles, on television, and in the movies. While a comprehensive list of all the materials used in the writing of this book would be prohibitive, some key sources include *Tourist News*, the *Sun*, the *Don Roger*, *National Geographic*, *St. Petersburg Register*, *St. Petersburg Independent*, and *Pinellas Review*. Additional information was obtained from the archives of the Don CeSar in the form of press releases, promotional materials and brochures, hotel newsletters and memos, and donated material from guests and residents of the past seventy-three years. A debt of gratitude is extended to all those—past, present, and future—who help preserve the Don for all generations to enjoy.